Worcestershire & the Malverns

Roger Noyce

COUNTRYSIDE BOOKS
NEWBURY BERKSHIRE

First published 2007
© Roger Noyce, 2007

COUNTRYSIDE BOOKS
3 Catherine Road
Newbury, Berkshire

To view our complete range of books,
please visit us at
www.countrysidebooks.co.uk

ISBN 978 1 84674 025 1

Photographs by the author and Margaret Noyce
Cover picture showing the Malvern Hills from across
the Teme Valley supplied by Bill Meadows

Maps by Gelder Design & Mapping

Designed by Peter Davies, Nautilus Design
Produced through MRM Associates Ltd, Reading
Printed by Cambridge University Press

Contents

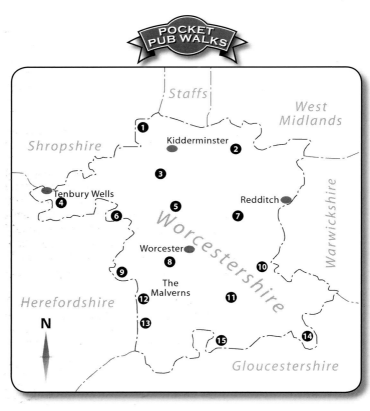

POCKET
PUB WALKS

Staffs

West
Midlands

Shropshire

❶

Kidderminster
❷

❸

Tenbury Wells
❹

❻

❺

Redditch
❼

Worcestershire

Warwickshire

Worcester
❽

❾

The
Malverns
❿

⓫

Herefordshire

⓬

⓭

⓮

⓯

N

Gloucestershire

Area map showing location of the walks

Introduction

The fifteen walks in this book seek to explore the timeless landscape of Worcestershire, with its feast of beauty, its historic buildings, its rolling countryside, its superb hills and its warm welcome. The routes are all between 3 and 6 miles in length and should be well within the capacity of the average person. They can be enjoyed equally by the casual or regular walker, being intended for an amble through delightful Worcestershire at a gentle pace with time to stand and stare and to experience some of the most beautiful views in the Midlands. Throughout Worcestershire there are welcoming black and white pubs that add to the pleasure of walking and there are many picturesque villages to visit.

The walking surface is generally very good so that people of mature years and families with young children should have little difficulty. None of the circuits in the book are inherently hazardous but sensible footwear should be worn. In dry weather the paths should be good under foot and normal outdoor footwear should be adequate. In wet weather or during the winter months, there could be some moist stretches of footpath, when it is preferable to wear stout waterproof boots or shoes – these give more protection to the ankle.

There can be few greater pleasures in life than to relax with a pint in hand after a pleasant country walk and to facilitate this each walk either starts from an attractive pub or passes near a named pub en route. Information on pub opening times is provided together with comments on food and drink – the pub telephone number is included to enable you to make enquiries before your visit. For a few of the walks, car parking is available at or near the pub but please be courteous and ask the publican if you want to leave your vehicle at the pub while out walking.

With each walk there is a sketch map of the route that is intended to identify the starting point for the walk and should be adequate to guide you for the walk. However, Ordnance Survey maps to the scale of 1:25,000 are specially designed for walkers and provide more detailed information. I recommend you to acquire the relevant Explorer maps and details of these are included with each walk. All of the routes incorporate public rights of way, where there is an onus upon every walker to look after our precious countryside and to protect the environment for future generations.

I am pleased to invite you to stroll the lovely footpaths around this beautiful area and to sample some of its finest inns. Enjoy yourself!

Roger Noyce

Publisher's Note

We hope that you obtain considerable enjoyment from this book; great care has been taken in its preparation. However, changes of landlord and actual closures are sadly not uncommon. Likewise, although at the time of publication all routes followed public rights of way or permitted paths, diversion orders can be made and permissions withdrawn.

We cannot, of course, be held responsible for such diversion orders and any inaccuracies in the text which result from these or any other changes to the routes, nor any damage which might result from walkers trespassing on private property. We are anxious though that all details covering the walks and pubs are kept up to date and would therefore welcome information from readers which would be relevant to future editions.

The simple sketch maps that accompany the walks in this book are based on notes made by the author whilst checking out the routes on the ground. However, for the benefit of a proper map, we do recommend that you purchase the relevant Ordnance Survey sheet covering your walk. The Ordnance Survey maps are widely available, especially through booksellers and local newsagents.

1 Shatterford

The Bellman's Cross Inn

Shatterford is part of the **Upper Arley parish**, which covers a mainly rural area of the Wyre Forest District in the north of Worcestershire. The river Severn flows through Upper Arley, and quite a large area to the west of the river forms part of the ancient Forest of Wyre. Shatterford, Pound Green and Upper Arley itself are the three villages which comprise the Upper Arley parish. Shatterford is well known for its lakes and wildlife park and the Bellman's Cross Inn. Pound Green has an ancient common and attracts cyclists and walkers to the forest glades and paths. Arley lies on the banks of the river, and welcomes large numbers of visitors, particularly to its church, the Arley arboretum, and the peaceful banks of the Severn. A particular feature of Upper Arley is the Severn Valley Railway, which runs along the west bank of the river Severn into Bewdley town. This easy stroll provides an opportunity to explore this beautiful area and to enjoy a super meal at the Bellman's Cross Inn.

Distance 3¼ miles.

OS Explorer 218 Wyre Forest and Kidderminster. GR 790811.

Undulating stroll along footpaths and good tracks.

Starting point The Bellman's Cross Inn, Shatterford.

How to get there Shatterford is a tiny village set 7 miles north-west of Kidderminster along the A442 (the Bridgnorth road). Park in the pub car park, with permission.

THE PUB The **Bellmans Cross Inn** at Shatterford is a large roadside country pub on the busy A442 that is well known throughout Worcestershire for its fine French cuisine. It serves a good range of traditional food, and fish is a speciality. Bar and restaurant food is available from baguettes to superb French meals. Real ales are served and there is a garden for the warmer months..

Opening times are from Monday to Saturday between 11 am and 3 pm and from 6 pm to 10 pm. On Sunday the opening hours are 12 noon to 3 pm and in the evening from 6 pm to 9.30 pm. Food is available during opening hours.
☎ *01299 861322*

1 Exit the inn car park at its rear and turn right. In a few yards turn left and go over a stile into pastureland. Follow the waymarker direction and walk to the right of a pond; then aim for the stile in the far left-hand corner of the field. Go over this stile and turn left to go over a further stile onto a track. Turn left and stroll up the track, passing a couple of country cottages. At the top of the

rise you will see a waymarker below. Walk down to this and turn right along a clear wide track. In 150 yards the track becomes a footpath and you reach the entrance to Cox's Coppice. Here you join the **North Worcestershire Path** by going over a stile and bearing slightly right onto its route and descending a lovely path through the woodland. It is a gentle descent and after about 500 yards of delightful walking you reach the wood end. Turn left to stay on the North Worcestershire Path and walk a fenced path along the edge of woodland. All too soon you arrive by a footbridge over a stream. The North Worcestershire Path and the Worcestershire Way cross this but you keep ahead going over a couple of stiles to arrive in open pastureland, with **Hollies Farm** up to your right. Proceed ahead along the left edge of the field until you see a waymarker on the left.

2 Turn right and stroll up the edge of the trees opposite, essentially following the route of the stream. Soon you will veer left, going

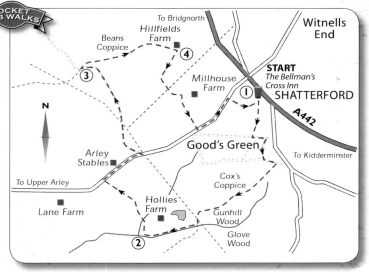

Along the track near Shatterford.

over a footbridge and stile to reach the other side of the stream. Follow the clear waymarkers by walking to the left of the field hedge; then go over a further stile and walk to the right of the hedge to the road. Turn right and stroll up the road, passing **Arley Stables**, and when you reach the next cottage turn left up a hedged track. This takes you past the cottages and beneath some overhead electric cabling. Initially it is a stone track that becomes a hedged grass track and then descends into woodland. The route arcs left and you go over a footbridge over a rather muddy area to continue along the track.

At a junction of tracks and footpaths, leave the track by going sharp right and follow the clear yellow public footpath waymarker. In a few yards the footpath divides into two and you veer off to the left. This path crosses back over another footbridge over a stream and soon you will be leaving Beans Coppice via a metal hand gate. Proceed past the end of the trees, looking out for a stile in the fence to the right – **Hillfields Farm** is visible to the left. This stile leads to the left of a farm cottage and a further stile.

Go over this stile and head right across pastureland to another stile in the right-hand field corner. At the next hedge bear left and aim for a stile in the fence opposite. This leads through a farm gate towards **Millhouse Farm**. Bear right and walk on the footpath to the right of the farm that exits onto the farm's entrance drive. Descend the driveway to the road on the edge of **Good's Green**. Turn left and walk along the pavement of the road for about 400 yards. Now cross over the road and head right along a wide farm track. When you reach a farm building turn left over the stile and bear left to arrive back at the **Bellman's Cross Inn**.

Places of interest nearby

Shatterford Wildlife Sanctuary and Fishery (to the south of Shatterford) is predominantly a fishery, although animals such as deer and natural wildlife are visible from the site.
☎ *01299 861597*

The **Severn Valley Railway** runs through Upper Arley so you could enjoy a trip on a steam train. The railway runs through 16 miles of wonderful countryside between Kidderminster and Bridgnorth.
☎ *01299 403816*

The Manchester Inn

The Waseley Hills form part of a range south of Birmingham and offer delightful views over the surrounding countryside and super walking for hikers and people just using them as a base to go exploring. It is an ideal place to park the car and go for a walk, being far enough outside Birmingham to appreciate the countryside and yet provides an alternative to nearby Lickey and Clent Hills. This pleasing short walk takes you from near the Manchester Inn into the Waseley Hills Country Park. You can call in at the visitor centre and will enjoy a super view from Windmill Hill overlooking Birmingham before turning southwards to see the Malvern Hills in the distance. The route continues along part of the Monarch's Way and later leads into delightful woodland where there are bluebells in the spring. A good track leads back to the inn for refreshments.

Distance 3¼ miles.

OS Explorer 219 Wolverhampton and Dudley. GR 964781.

Starting point The Manchester Inn.

Undulating walk with one main hill.

How to get there *The Waseley Hills are about 8 miles west of Birmingham. From Junction 4 of the M5, follow the A491 to Stourbridge. Turn right into Money Lane (B4551) – you will see a brown country park sign. Carry straight on until you see the Manchester Inn on your left – parking is opposite.*

THE PUB Although part of the building was erected in around 1830, the **Manchester Inn** did not become a pub until about 1970. This attractive inn is well frequented by walkers in the area and gives a warm welcome, with home-cooked food and a selection of cask ales. All of the food is reasonably priced and you can enjoy it in the beer garden that overlooks the hills. There is a roast available on Sundays when the caramel apple cobbler served with fresh cream is a favourite.

Opening times are from 11.30 am to 11 pm every day except Sunday when it opens at noon and closes at 10.30 pm. Food is available between noon and 3 pm and between 6 pm and 10 pm. On Sunday food is available at lunchtime only, between noon and 4 pm.
☎ *01562 710242 Website: www.nicelittlepub.co.uk*

1 Leave the car park and head left along the B4551 road. In about 50 yards turn left up the lane which will take you over the M5 and to a junction. Turn left and stroll up the lane through the hamlet of **Chapman's Hill**. At the end of the hamlet the lane bends right; just after this bear right to go through the hand gate into pastureland. Turn left, walking the clear footpath inside the field hedge until you reach a stile and an entrance to **Waseley Hills Country Park**. Turn left and descend the slope to the park's visitor centre.

2 Leave the visitor centre via the kissing gate and head up to the steps ahead. These will lead you up to the topograph on **Windmill Hill**, from where you will enjoy a most superb view over Birmingham. Bear left and join the main path – the **North Worcestershire Path**. Follow the clear signs and you will pass

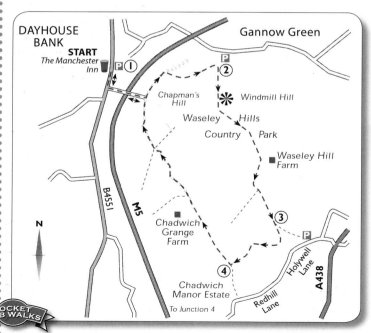

close to a plantation of trees and descend to another kissing gate – some 600 yards of delightful walking. You pass by the end of an area of woodland and then ascend to another kissing gate. Ignore the **Monarch's Way** waymarker and continue up the **North Worcestershire Path** until it bends left and descends into woodland towards a parking area.

Continue ahead along the signed footpath, walking to the right of the hedge. The path arcs right and immediately after passing the Waseley Country Park sign (there is a bench opposite) turn left over a stile and follow the **Monarch's Way**, walking to the right of the field hedge.

Just before reaching a driveway, turn right and head towards a stile into woodland. Follow the footpath through the trees – you can expect to enjoy bluebells in spring – and exit over another stile onto open land. Walk the footpath across the land to reach a stile set to the right of **Chadwich Grange Farm**. Turn right along a good wide track and after about ½ mile of attractive walking you will reach the end of **Chapman's Hill**. Turn left and retrace your steps over the M5 to return to the start.

Places of interest nearby

Nearby **Clent Hills** include 440 acres of woodland and heathland managed by the National Trust. Perhaps add to a day out in the area and call in at the Clent Visitor Centre.
Website: www.nationaltrust.org.uk

Woodgate Valley Country Park (9 miles to the north-west) comprises 450 acres of meadows, hedgerows and woodland, with the Bourn Brook running through its centre – it is an ideal place to observe wildlife.
Website: www.birmingham.gov.uk

3 Stourport-on-Severn

The Bay Horse Inn

Wilden is a small village set on the outskirts of Stourport-on-Severn. Stourport remains an industrial town known for its carpet manufacturing and has the largest chainworks in Europe, but is best known as a place of pilgrimage for canal lovers. Here, the river Stour meets the river Severn and the Staffordshire and Worcester Canal commences its journey to link up with the Trent and Mersey Canal at Great Haywood. The canal is the realisation of the dream of an illiterate farmer's son called James Brindley, who came to Worcestershire in 1756, and the rest is history. A visit to the basin in Stourport is a delight of colourful inland watercraft. The Georgian charm remains, with the original long redbrick warehouse and white clock tower. This easy walk starts in nearby Hartlebury Common that enjoys fine views over the town and the nearby countryside. The walk takes you to see the Staffordshire and Worcestershire Canal and up an old railway track into pleasing countryside. The descent into lovely Charlton is a treat and you return through the common.

THE PUB The **Bay Horse Inn**, a lovely old welcoming inn, has original woodwork and bare brick walls, and is adorned with colourful flowers in summer. Guest ales are changed weekly and Strongbow cider is also on tap. Wines can be taken by the glass or by the bottle. All meals are made from fresh foods, with fish and chicken dishes being particular favourites. The Sunday roast is very popular, so it is advisable to book ahead.

Opening times are from 11 am to 11 pm every day except Sunday when it closes at 10.30 pm. Food is available between 12 noon to 2 pm (to 3 pm on Saturday and Sunday) and from 6.30 pm to 9 pm (9.30 pm on Saturday and from 7 pm to 9 pm on Sunday).
☎ *01299 822238*

Distance 4 miles.

OS Explorer 218 Kidderminster & Wyre Forest GR 824715.

Easy walk along footpaths and good tracks.

Starting point Wilden Top car park, Hartlebury Common.

How to get there *Stourport-on-Severn is 4 miles south of Kidderminster. Wilden Top car park is on Hartlebury Common, off the A4193 road.*

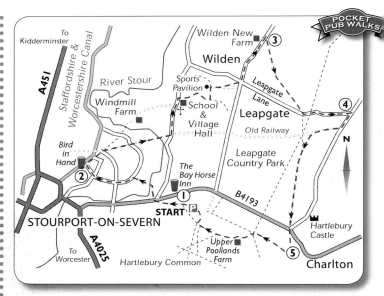

1 From the car park head towards the top left-hand corner of the common. Exit onto the fairly quiet B4193 road and turn left. Immediately after crossing **Wilden Lane**, turn right up a lane signed to **Mitton Mill Industrial Estate**. Follow the lane over the **river Stour** to a road junction and turn left along a residential road. After crossing the road island continue ahead. Where the road bends sharp left, go right up a narrow road (the left-hand one of two) and ascend to the left of the **Bird in Hand** public house. Turn right along a passageway at the back of the pub to arrive on the towpath of the **Staffordshire and Worcestershire Canal**.

2 Turn right along the towpath and pass beneath a bridge. Then ascend right up onto the **Leapgate Old Railway**. Turn left and after about 550 yards descend steps to the right to reach **Wilden Lane**. Turn left along the pavement for about 600 yards, passing **All Saints church** and then a school and the village hall. Turn

sharp right up a dead end lane and after passing the entrance to the **Old Vicarage** ascend the stepped path to a football ground. Head right around the edge of the playing area, going left at the field corner and passing to the right of the pavilion to a lane. Turn right along the lane and soon bear left diagonally crossing a 'private field'. Exit onto the road at a road junction and head up the lane opposite, passing an attractive housing estate. Soon you pass an impressive house called **The Oaks** and **New Wilden Farm**. Continue up the lane for a further 50 yards.

3 Turn right over the field corner stile, following the waymarker over a mid-field stile. Now aim for a stile set to the left of a large oak tree. Aim to the left of the buildings of **Leapgate Farm**

The Staffordshire and Worcestershire Canal, Stourport.

and go left through the new metal hand-gate, crossing a field to a second hand-gate. Turn right to a final gate to reach a quiet country lane. Head left along the lane for almost 500 yards to a junction.

4 Turn right and in about 100 yards go right again to rejoin the Leapgate Old Railway line. In about 300 yards you will reach a railway bridge and turn left through the farm gate onto a good wide track – in just under ½ mile you reach the B4193 road at **Charlton**. Cross the B4193 and head down the quiet lane opposite, walking to the left of the impressive **Charlton Coach House** and passing a number of attractive properties. Soon you reach a junction of footpaths.

5 Turn right but do not enter the private garden. Instead ascend a footpath into a bank of trees, passing to the right of a greenhouse into open countryside. The footpath is set to the right of fencing and soon you will see **Upper Poollands Farm** in the dip ahead. Bear right to the field hedge and descend the steps of the waymarked path, ascending the next field to a farm gate. Turn left through this gate, bearing right to a gate by the large barn. Continue ahead between farm buildings to a waymarked gate. Head up the side of the field, passing through horse pasture to reach a final gate onto **Hartlebury Common**. Follow the route ahead through the common and soon you will see parked cars through the trees to your right.

Places of interest nearby

Hartlebury Castle was for centuries the home of the Bishops of Worcester. The red-stone mansion was originally built in 1675 but was restored in 1964 and today houses the Worcestershire County Museum, exhibiting local crafts and industries.
☎ *01299 250416*

Pembroke House

Tenbury Wells is a market town set on the banks of the river Teme and surrounded by apple orchards and hop fields. A saline spring was discovered in the town in 1838 and this brought about the building of a pump room at the rear of Crow Hotel in 1862 (now restored as Tenbury Spa). The Pump Rooms and the many half-timbered and Georgian houses are a great fascination to visitors. The walk takes you around the attractive spa town of Tenbury Wells and along quiet footpaths and country lanes.

THE PUB Built in about 1580, **Pembroke House** was originally a toll house, being on the road to Worcester. The snug is a melange of shire brass, stuffed animal heads, old cider tankards and chintz. You will find real ales and a wide selection of wines, that can be taken by the bottle or by glass. Steaks, cod and gammon are very popular with visitors and locals alike and there is an attractive bar snack menu for anyone in a hurry. Look out for the chicken curry and the chilli, while on Sunday there is the traditional roast lunch to enjoy. The menu is excellent and the quality is extremely high.

Opening times on weekdays are from noon to 2.30 pm and 6 pm to 11 pm and all day on Saturdays and Sundays. During the daytime, food is available from noon to 2 pm throughout the week. In the evenings the food hours are from 6 pm to 8 pm Monday to Saturday, but no food is served on Sunday evening.
☎ *01584 810301*

Distance 4½ miles.

OS Explorer 203 Ludlow GR 597684.

A walk on footpaths, with one hill to negotiate.

Starting point The car park near the swimming pool by Burgage recreation ground

How to get there *Tenbury Wells is situated about 18 miles west of Kidderminster (22 miles north-west of Worcester) and is best approached on the A456 Worcester road crossing over the Teme Bridge into the town. The car park is signed on the left.*

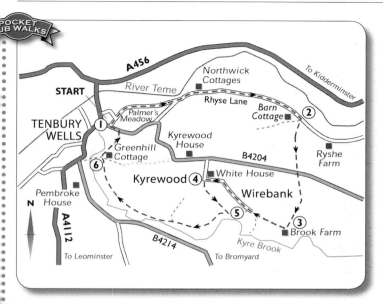

1 From the car park walk past the swimming pool and go right on the footpath to the right of **Kyre Brook**. After about ¼ mile you will pass the town's rugby fields and in a just over a further ½ mile will arrive at **Rhyse Lane**, which you should walk along for the next 1¼ miles.

2 Just after passing **Barn Cottage**, turn right through a farm gate, passing to the right of a large barn, then ascend a fairly steep track to the right of woodland. The ascent of some 350 yards leads to a stile at the top of the hill. Go over the stile and continue ahead, keeping to the left of the hedge until you reach a stile onto the B4204 road. Cross over the road and go through the gate opposite, descending pastureland to go over the footbridge by a waymarker. Continue along the waymarked path to the right of woodland and soon you will arrive on **Brook Drive**, near **Brook Farm**.

The Pump Room at Tenbury Wells.

[3] Turn right along the farm drive that becomes a tarmac lane, passing by **Wirebank Cottage** and reaching a lane junction by **White House**.

[4] Turn left along the lane and then bear right into the drive of a farm complex at **Kyrewood**. Proceed between the farm buildings, bearing left, then right, and passing through a farm gate onto a farm track. Descend the track, which arcs gently right then left as you leave the farm. At the bottom of the track go over a stile, bearing right, and walk along the pastureland to the left of and

below **New Court**. Proceed over a stile onto the house driveway, going left for about 100 yards.

Turn right over the hedge stile at the entrance to the house drive and walk on the clear path to the left of woodland for about ½ mile. You will see houses to your left on the other side of **Kyre Brook** as you progress in a general north-westerly direction, continuing past the attractive **Greenhill Cottage** to a stile in the field hedge.

Go over the stile and turn right (if you meander to the left, you will see stepping stones over the brook). Follow a clear path that leads up through the trees onto a fenced footpath and the B4204 road in **Tenbury Wells**. Turn left across the bridge over **Kyre Brook**; then head right on a footpath by the side of the brook and you will soon arrive back in the car park.

Places of interest nearby

The **Pump Rooms**, passed at the end of the walk, were designed by James Cranston of Birmingham and are one of the earliest examples of prefabrication (the sheets were made in Birmingham and assembled on site). They were built in 1862 by the Tenbury Improvement Company and form a distinctive feature in the town.
☎ *01584 819345*

Enjoy a pleasant day in the 29 acres of mature grounds of **Kyre Park**, ¾ mile to the west. There is a Norman dovecote, a Jacobean tithe barn, and waterfalls and lakes to explore.
☎ *01885 410247*

Burford House (Tenbury Wells) is a beautiful Georgian house and art gallery, with superb gardens along the banks of the River Teme.
☎ *01584 810777*

The Honeybee Inn

Doverdale is an ancient small parish situated north-west of Droitwich where the Elmley or Doverdale Brook forms a boundary between Ombersley and Doverdale. The church of St Mary the Virgin dates from the 12th century and was built on the site of an earlier Saxon church. This delightful easy walk starts from near the church and takes you into lovely Worcestershire countryside, walking along part of the Wychavon/Monarch's Way before passing through attractive woodland. The route concludes up a farm track and then passes near to Doverdale Mill.

Distance 5 miles.

OS Explorer 204 Worcester and Droitwich Spa. GR 861659.

Starting point The car park of St Mary's church, Doverdale.

Easy walking, including part of the Wychavon Way.

How to get there *Doverdale is about 5 miles north-west of Droitwich. Leave Droitwich on the A442. Turn left in Hampton Lovett and follow the signs to Doverdale, then turn left to reach the church.*

HE UB The **Honeybee Inn** is situated in spectacular rolling countryside. This is Britain's only honey farm pub, where honey is actually produced on the premises, and has been for at least 900 years. The plethora of honey-making memorabilia from centuries past which adorns this delightfully appointed pub will enthral all the family. Honeycomb ale is always available, in addition to a menu that offers many delicious dishes made with all types of honey. In the interior workshop the honey extraction process takes place, while inside the inn there is a huge range of honey and related items available for purchase. Dozens of large hives are scattered around the outside of the inn, with at least a dozen or more active at any one time, mostly near the pool at the bottom of the hill.

Opening times are 11.30 am to 11 pm Monday to Saturday; 12 noon to 10.30 pm on Sunday. Food is available all week between 12 noon and 10 pm.
☎ *01299 851620*

1 Leave the church car park to reach the lane. Turn right and in about 25 yards turn left over a stile into a cultivated field. Head towards the trees and go over a stile and footbridge into a narrow strip of woodland, following the waymarker, and cross over the next field. Head for the hedge gap opposite. Follow the footsteps of those who have walked the path before and aim for the hedge situated south of **Pakington Farm**. Walk by the side of the hedge to a farm track and turn right. At the bottom of the field turn left and follow the footpath that hugs the left field hedge; this arcs gently right. At the end of the field turn right. Halfway up the next hedge, turn left along the clear waymarked farm track by the side of a cultivated field. Continue ahead at the junction of paths and ascend the field, aiming for its far right-hand corner.

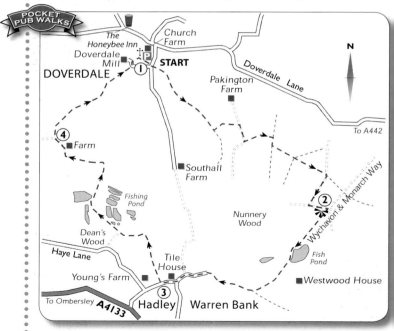

Swans on the fishing lake.

Turn right to walk along the farm track. In about 300 yards you will reach a track junction. Turn left and walk to another junction of footpaths.

Turn right through the gate and stroll down the wide footpath towards **Nunnery Wood**. You are now walking the **Wychavon/ Monarch's Way**. A good footpath leads through the woodland and you pass a fishing lake – to your left. Exit the wood via the metal gate and bear right to continue along the **Monarch's Way**. A farm gate allows access onto a fenced path, where you turn right. Ascend past the stable block, passing to the left of **Nunnery Wood**. At its end bear right and descend the fenced footpath to the left of the trees to reach the hamlet of **Hadley**. You pass by the old mill and continue up the quiet country road. At the road junction bear right to continue past **Tile House**.

Worcestershire & the Malverns

[3] In about 125 yards turn right over a stile and cross pastureland to go through a farm gateway – the football pitch of Hadley Rangers is to your left. Continue towards the next farm gate but about 15 yards before reaching this turn right over a stile and turn left along the side of the field hedge. After passing a narrow strip of trees, cross the field to a waymarker post. Turn left along the grass track and in about 250 yards enter **Dean's Wood**. Initially the footpath is along the right edge of the trees, with fishing pools to your right. Continue into the woodland and, in another 200 yards, you reach the main fishing pool. Turn right along the edge of the pool and at its next corner look out for a path going off to the right into the trees. Head over the footbridge and proceed through the woodland, exiting via a couple of stiles. Cross over the cultivated field and go over the stile opposite into more woodland before emerging in pastureland; then turn sharp left. At the end of the field go through the gate and along the track past a farm. Continue along the track for the next 100 yards.

[4] Where the driveway bends sharp left, turn right over the hedge stile onto a footpath. The path arcs right and soon you will be walking by a tree-lined brook. At the next field corner turn left into the trees and you will then emerge into the open. Follow the waymarker aiming towards the church of St Mary in **Doverdale**. At the lane turn left and then go immediately right over a stile. Cross the pastureland, bearing right to enter the churchyard via a final stile.

Places of interest nearby

Ombersley (approximately 4 miles south-west) is one of the famous black and white villages of Worcestershire and it is a delight to walk round and to see its 14th-century plague stone.

6 Clifton upon Teme

The Lion Inn

Situated about a mile away from the river Teme, Clifton upon Teme is a picturesque village of black and white cottages mingled with cottages of grey stone, timber and red brick. The post office is rendered white with black beams, and the occasional Georgian façade adds a touch of elegance to the beautiful village. The church of St Kenelm is situated next to the 12th-century Lion Inn, and was named after the county's own boy saint, who was murdered at the tender age of seven in AD 819. Its superb spire is clad in Canadian cedarwood shingles and is topped by a golden cockerel weather vane. Inside look for the effigy of a cross-legged, 13th-century knight, with his feet resting on a dog. This is Ralph de Wysham, a crusader who

Worcestershire & the Malverns

Distance 5 miles.

OS Explorer 204 Worcester and Droitwich Spa. GR 714615.

Starting point The village green in Clifton upon Teme.

Undulating walk, with lovely views.

How to get there Clifton upon Teme is situated 9½ miles south-east of Tenbury Wells along the B4204 road. Park with consideration on the green.

once lived in nearby Woodmanton Manor. This walk offers the opportunity to admire the lovely village and to enjoy the surrounding unspoiled countryside and nearby villages in what is mainly a conservation area.

THE PUB The 12th-century **Lion Inn** was originally the guildhall or village meeting house. It was also once referred to as the manor house and used as a local court house. The picturesque inn is adorned with lovely flower baskets throughout the summer and is the focal point for the community. The inn has won many awards for its fine food. The daily specials board and lunchtime gourmet events attract visitors and locals alike.

Opening times are Monday to Thursday noon to 3 pm and 6 pm to midnight, Friday and Saturday 11 am to 3 pm and 5 pm to 1 am; Sunday noon to 11.30 pm. Food is served from noon to 2 pm and 6 pm to 9 pm Monday to Saturday. Sunday roasts are available if booked in advance. No food is available on Sunday evenings.
☎ *01886 812975*

Clifton upon Teme

1 From the village green walk to the right past the **Lion Inn**.

2 Within 50 yards turn left at a footpath sign up a residential drive opposite **The Old Forge**. **St Kenelm's church** is just past the driveway. Head up the driveway, passing the garage onto a track that leads to a stile. Go over the stile and continue along a clear path by the field hedge, going over a further stile in the corner. Cross over the next field aiming for another stile set in the far corner, to the left of and beyond **Church House Farm**. Turn right over this stile and cross the field (using the bridge) to another stile and a good farm track. Turn left and soon you approach a field hedge, with a super view embracing the **Malvern Hills** and the **Cotswold Hills**, with **Broadway Tower** on the horizon. Descend the track by the left field hedge, passing by a copse and woodland. Continue ahead down the path, passing to the right of **Slashes Coppice**. Eventually you pass through an area of trees and walk along the right edge of the woodland to a gate onto a track in the trees. Maintain your line and descend over a ditch.

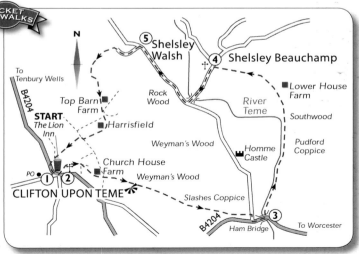

St Kenelm's church, Clifton.

Then continue by the side of the hedge to arrive on the road near **Ham House** and **Old Barn Cottage**. Turn right along the road to reach the B4204 road, then go left over **Ham Bridge** (over the river Teme).

3 About 40 yards beyond the bridge turn left onto a footpath that hugs the bank of the river over several fields and stiles. The winding path passes a spring and then goes to the left of trees. Once clear of the woodland the path crosses over several farm fields, with **Lower House Farm** up to your right. After about

1½ miles you arrive at a road opposite **All Saints' church** in **Shelsley Beauchamp**.

Turn left and cross over **New Mill Bridge** to reach the main road. Turn right along the side of this usually quiet road towards the village of **Shelsley Walsh**.

Turn left up a lane into the village; then bear right between **St Andrew's church** and **Court Farm House**. Now turn left up a private road which is the famous hill climb of the Midlands Automobile Club where Raymond Mays made his name. This fairly steep tarmac lane ascends through the trees and continues up past **Top Barn Farm**. Pass through the gate by the barn and continue along the lane until you reach an attractive cottage called **Harrisfield**. Here, turn right, joining a footpath that veers past the cottage, to soon cross over a footbridge where the path becomes a hedge track. At its top turn right along a footpath coming in from the left and in about 100 yards pause to enjoy the view behind you of **Abberley Hill** and its landmark clock tower. Continue by the side of the field hedge; go through the farm gate, walking over pastureland and along a hedged path to arrive at the B4204 road in **Clifton upon Teme**. Turn left past an attractive cottage, the post office and a number of black and white houses to arrive back at the village green.

Places of interest nearby

Witley Court, 4 miles north-east, is a former country house, now owned by English Heritage. Once one of the finest houses in the England, it suffered a serious fire in 1937 and was abandoned. The parish church (not English Heritage) has super stained-glass windows and baroque architecture. The superb parkland has largely been restored and offers wonderful Italian gardens.
☎ *01299 896636*

The Rose & Crown

Feckenham is a picturesque village with a lovely village green, two busy family-run pubs and two active parish churches. The surrounding countryside is idyllic and there is a nature reserve at nearby Wylde Moor, where you can see a glorious selection of wild flowers, insects and birds. The main parish church, the church of St John the Baptist, stands proud on a hill in the village and is fascinating to visit. The churchyard is of particular interest. The old churchyard cross is 19th-century but the base and the steps are medieval. Below the east window of the church are three ancient memorials dating from 1662, 1675 and 1676. Perhaps the most interesting item is the memorial to a gypsy lady, Phoebe Lee, who died in 1861. This memorial is set within railings to the north of the church. Phoebe was said to be the Queen of the Gypsies and a huge gathering of travellers attended

Distance 5½ miles.

OS Explorer 204 Worcester and Droitwich Spa, and 220 Birmingham. GR 009614.

Starting point The village car park in Feckenham.

Easy walk along good paths and tracks. One hill to negotiate.

How to get there *Feckenham is about 9 miles south of Redditch. Leave Redditch on the A441 road. In Astwood Bank turn right at the road junction and Astwood Lane will lead you into Feckenham. After passing the Rose and Crown turn right into the car park.*

the burial service. This easy walk takes you through part of a nature reserve and onto Berrow Hill for a fine view of the area.

THE PUB The **Rose and Crown** is situated in the middle of Feckenham and is a regular haunt of rambling groups. There are always two real ales on tap and these are changed every few months. You can select from the usual range of bar snacks that include a superb BLT or perhaps indulge yourself with a gammon steak. Vegetarian options are also available.

Opening times during the week are between 11 am and 3 pm (noon to 4 pm on Saturday) and from 6 pm until 11 pm. On Sunday it is open from noon until 4 pm and from 7 pm to 10.30 pm. Food is available between noon and 2 pm each day, and between 7 pm and 9 pm and 6 pm to 9 pm on Saturday and Sunday respectively.
☎ *01527 892188*

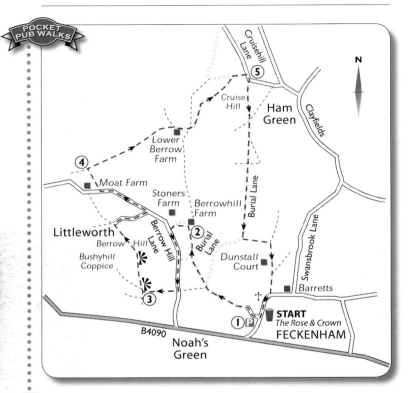

1 Leave the car park, turning left past a small housing estate, and pass the sports ground. Bear right into the main square and then turn left down **Mill Lane**. You will soon pass the old water mill and then arc right over a footbridge to ascend the clear track up through woodland. Near its top the track bends left but here you proceed ahead and continue up the clear footpath that leads you into the grounds of **Berrowhill Farm**.

2 Follow the waymarker that points left and descend the driveway to the farm to reach **Berrow Hill Lane**. Turn left and stroll along

this quiet lane for about ½ mile; then turn right over a stile and ascend to the top of **Berrow Hill** to enjoy a very fine view.

After reaching a junction of footpaths at the top, turn right, heading along the crest of the hill to continue to enjoy those super views over **Feckenham** to the right. After passing the trig point (109m) you soon reach a stile into woodland. Descend the footpath through the trees for about 200 yards, passing to the left of a lovely cottage, and eventually you will reach a junction of paths. Here, turn right along a footpath set to the left of the cottage, and soon you will reach the roadway that leads to **Berrow Hill Lane**. Head left up the lane for about 500 yards, then turn right up a clearly signed track set to the right of **Moat Farm**. You go over several stiles until you reach a junction of paths.

The Green at Feckenham.

4. Here, turn right and walk the footpath set to the left of the field hedge. In about ½ mile you will reach **Lower Berrow Farm**, where you turn right between the farm buildings and emerge on the driveway. Walk along this driveway enjoying the fine view behind you. All too soon you bear right to reach **Cruisehill Lane**.

5. Turn right and head down the lane for about 450 yards, then turn right up a driveway and descend a track called **Burial Lane**, going generally southwards. Walk down the track for about a mile until it arcs gently right. Here, look out for a stile going off to the left and turn left. In 275 yards turn right and walk down the clear footpath that takes you to the left of **Dunstall Court**, which you will see off to your right. In about 550 yards you will arrive on the pavement in **Feckenham**. Bear right and stroll through the fine churchyard of St John to see the gravestone of Phoebe Lee, 'Queen of the Gypsies'. Continue through the churchyard and exit via the lychgate. Continue ahead and you will reach the village green. Bear right and then go left to retrace your steps back to the car parking area.

Places of interest nearby

Whilst here, why not call into the well-known outdoor store of **Barretts of Feckenham** and take a look at their huge range of walking gear and camping equipment.
☎ *01527 892935 Website: www.barretsoutdoor.co.uk*

The Three Nuns Inn

Collett's Green is a small village set near the banks of the river Teme and the village of Powick. It is south of Powick Bridge, where the famous Battle of Worcester took place in 1651. By Powick Bridge is an old building which, at the beginning of the 20th century, was the first hydroelectric power station in England, producing DC electricity for Worcester and Malvern. The nearby riverside inn by the main bridge in Worcester was called the Old Rectifying House; here the electricity was converted to AC for the city. The power station was eventually replaced by a large flour mill and has since been converted into private residences. This easy walk takes you from the village of Collett's Green for some excellent views over the nearby Malvern Hills. You will be walking in lovely Worcestershire countryside on a route that finishes with a walk up through the delightful Lord's Wood, where wildlife can often be seen.

THE PUB Walkers are guaranteed a warm welcome at the **Three Nuns Inn**, where Marston's Bitter and Banks's Mild are the two main real ales to enjoy. Strongbow cider is on draught, as is Guinness. A full menu of appetising offerings includes the local favourites of mixed grill and home-cooked ham. Booking is required for Sunday lunch if you do not wish to be disappointed.

Opening times are from noon to 2 pm and 6 pm to 11 pm (7 pm to 10.30 pm on Sundays). Food is available every day except Sunday evening, from noon to 2 pm and from 6.30 pm to 8.30 pm.
☎ *01905 830442*

Distance 4 miles.

OS Explorer 204 Worcester and Droitwich. GR 818513.

Starting point The Three Nuns Inn, Collett's Green.

Easy walk, with good views.

How to get there *Collett's Green is 2½ miles south-west of Worcester. Approach from Worcester along the A449 road. At the large roundabout take the fourth turning right into Collett's Green to find the Three Nuns Inn.*

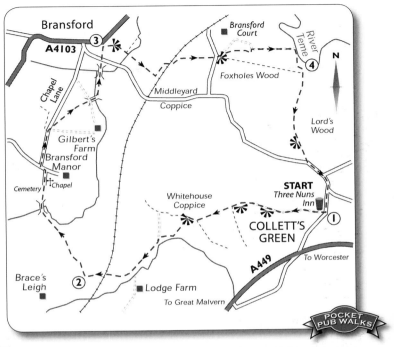

Exit the car park at the **Three Nuns** and turn right and right again immediately after the inn along the waymarked track. Turn right over the stile into pastureland, walking to the right of the field hedge for about 550 yards. After passing a house up to the right, turn left through a kissing gate into a large field for a super view towards the **Malvern Hills**. Continue along the wide path to the left of the hedge, bearing right between the trees of **Whitehouse Coppice**. Turn left, joining a footpath that emerges from the coppice, and descend the field, aiming towards a farm gate in its bottom left-hand corner – **Lodge Farm** is up to the left. Do not go through the farm gate but turn right by the field hedge and a stream. Turn right at the waymarker post and ascend

St Edburga's chapel.

to a stile in the opposite hedge. Cross the bridge over the railway line and head towards the stile in the fence ahead. **Brace's Leigh** is ahead.

2 Turn right, away from **Brace's Leigh**, to a stile in the field corner. Continue to the left of the hedge in the next field and in about 150 yards go right over a pair of stiles. Walk left to the far end of this long field – there is a stream over to the right. At the field end bear right across the bridge over the stream and ascend to the left of the field hedge. A stile leads to a lane that descends past the **Chapel of St Edburga**. Continue past the entrance to **Bransford**

Hall; then turn right at the road junction and walk along **Chapel Lane** for about 300 yards. Turn right over a field corner stile, aiming towards the field's far corner – the **Oast House** is to the right. Cross a stile leading onto a farm track. Pass to the left of a residence and through a farm gate over a stream. Bear left, passing through the far hedge gap to arrive at a stile onto a lane. Cross over the lane and head up the next field to a stile.

3 Do not go over this stile but turn right, descending the hill towards a footbridge. Continue to the left of the field hedge to arrive at the railway line. Turn left just before the fenced-off area and in about 150 yards turn right, ascending to a pair of stiles, and cross the line. Turn left and then go right up the field edge to a stile onto a lane. Cross the lane and bear right over another stile into the large grass area next to **Bransford Court**. Walk on the permissive footpath and bear left and then right onto the rear driveway to the **Court**. In about 400 yards the good track bends right and you reach a bench seat above the **river Teme** – near an entrance gate.

4 Pass through the gate and turn right, walking to the left of fencing to a stile into **Lord's Wood**. Proceed up the well-walked footpath through the delightful woodland. The footpath veers left out of the trees and soon you will be walking past a house to reach a road. Turn left along the quiet road that bends left. Then you bear right, passing the sign for **Powick**. At the next junction turn right up the **Malvern road** to return to the **Three Nuns Inn**.

Places of interest nearby

Leigh Court Barn (2 miles north-west) is the largest timber-framed 14th-century barn in Britain. It was built for the monks of Pershore Abbey and is maintained by English Heritage. Admission is free.
☎ *0870 333 1181*

The Nelson Inn

Suckley is a delightful small village that is well known for its fruit and for the growing of hops. On this walk you pass through fruit orchards and may see apples being prepared for the famous Bulmers cider factory. The walk takes you along part of the Worcestershire Way, where a super track leads over Suckley Hill; the Suckley section of the path is in the Malvern Hills Area of Outstanding Natural Beauty. The Worcestershire Way was opened in 1989 by what was then the Hereford and Worcester County Council. In 2004 the Worcestershire Way was relaunched in truncated form, with sections removed that had previously strayed into Herefordshire. The 2004 route is 31 miles long and runs between Bewdley and the Malvern Hills. The Way links the Staffordshire Way and the North Worcestershire Path with the Malvern Hills.

Distance 3½ miles.

OS Explorer 204 Worcester and Droitwich Spa. GR 721516.

Starting point Suckley church.

Undulating walk along good paths and forest tracks. One hill.

How to get there *Suckley is 16 miles south-west of Worcester. Best approached on the A1043 Hereford road. Leave this at Bransford and follow the road signs to Suckley. In Suckley follow the signs to the church.*

THE PUB The **Nelson Inn** is a family-run freehouse, with log fires and traditional ales. You are assured of quality home-cooked food that, in summer, can be enjoyed in the patio garden. Three roasts are on offer each Sunday lunchtime and, on Tuesdays and Thursdays, there are special lunches for OAPs. Look out for the daily specials.

Opening times during the week are from noon to 2.30 pm (not Monday lunchtime) and from 7 pm until 11 pm (6 pm to 11 pm on Friday and Saturday). Sunday opening is noon until 3 pm and from 7 pm to 10.30 pm. Food is available at lunchtime, and in the evenings from 7 pm onwards. Food is also available on Sunday evenings from 7 pm to 9.30 pm.
☎ *01886 884530*

From **Suckley church** stroll down to the main road. Turn left and in a few yards go right over a stile, following the waymarker direction to a footbridge over the stream. Pass to the right of

Worcestershire & the Malverns

the pond. Then head up the field to a metal hand gate and a stile. Pass to the right of the storage building and continue ahead over pastureland, keeping by the field hedge. At the end of the second field head right, over a stile and over a cultivated field, to a long footbridge. Cross over the footbridge and bear left through a hand gate. The route now starts an ascent up towards the trees on **Suckley Hill**. Enter the trees via a stile and proceed up through the wood on the clear footpath – this is a fairly steep but short ascent.

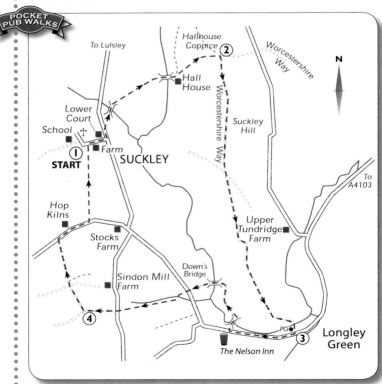

The Worcestershire countryside.

2 At the top of the hill you will reach a junction of footpaths and forest tracks. Turn right along the track and then turn right again, following the **Worcestershire Way** path going southwards through **Suckley Wood** – **do not** take the Worcestershire Way track that arcs left and goes northwards. Walk on this good track through **Suckley Wood** for the next 1½ miles. Eventually you will exit the trees through a hand gate and descend pastureland, with **Upper Tundridge Farm** to your far left. After going through a pair of metal hand gates you will walk up a hedged footpath to arrive on the main road in **Longley Green**.

3 Turn right and stroll past the village post office. After walking along the side of the generally quiet road for about 500 yards, you will see the **Nelson Inn** on the left. Just before reaching the drive to the inn turn right and go over a stile. The path arcs right to a footbridge. Go over this and turn left along a wide track. Pass through the farm gate and walk on the track below some hedged houses with the **Leigh Brook** to the left. The track bends right and you walk up the side of fencing towards a farm complex. Turn left and go through the hand gate onto the driveway to the farmhouse. Walk down this driveway and go over **Downs Bridge**. Soon you will reach the main road again. Here turn left and then go immediately right through a farm gate. In a few yards, turn left over a stile and bear right so as to walk on the other side of the hedge along a wide footpath set to the right of hop fencing. In the next field you may wish to walk around the edge of the hop trellis to a stile in the far hedge. Go over this and cross over the road onto a lane, with more hop fencing to your left. Walk up this lane for about 200 yards.

4 Turn right at the bend in the lane and you will soon reach a junction of footpaths and an apple processing area. Continue ahead, with apple trees to your left for about 350 yards, until you reach a road. Turn right and walk past the hop kilns. About 120 yards beyond the hop kilns turn left through a farm gateway and take the signed footpath set to the left of the field hedge. There is a nice view of the hop kilns to your left and ahead there is a pleasing view of Suckley church and the lovely Worcestershire countryside. Continue to the left of the field hedge and soon you will emerge via another farm gateway at the parking area by **Suckley church**.

Places of interest nearby

The Malvern Hills are a must-visit 'mountain range in miniature' with the highest point being the Worcestershire Beacon (425m). Walking the ridge crest is a special treat, with wonderful views as far as Wales and the Cotswolds. The Malvern ridge boasts three ancient hill forts, the most famous being the ditches and ramparts of British Camp.

The Coach & Horses

Harvington village is a historic treasure waiting to be discovered. Way back in 2,000 BC, a fine bronze celt (an ancient cleaving instrument) was found in the watering ditch between Harvington and Salford Priors. Harvington appeared in the Domesday Book of 1086 as Hereforton when there were just three hides each paying taxes (hides comprised 60 to 120 acres of land, each supporting one family). For many years the main Stratford to Evesham road passed through the middle of the village, causing traffic problems. Eventually the A435 bypass was built and Harvington recaptured its rural appearance, retaining a number of very attractive half-timbered and thatched properties. The parish church dominates the old part of the village and in the 13th century was more of a social centre – on high days and holidays the church was filled with with merchandise, stalls and stall holders. This pleasant short walk takes you through the surrounding fruit farms to nearby Atch Lench and its delightful

Distance 6 miles.

OS Explorer 205 Stratford-upon-Avon and Evesham.
GR 052493.

Starting point The lay-by near to Myatt's Field.

An easy walk, with one short hill to negotiate.

How to get there *Leave the A46 at the Bidford-on-Avon roundabout and head along the B435 road towards Harvington. In about 2 miles turn right up the old Stratford road to reach the Coach & Horses public house. Turn right up Station Road and in about ½ mile you will see the lay-by on the left.*

thatched cottages and then passes through the old part of Harvington village.

THE PUB The **Coach & Horses** is an attractive village pub, opposite the church, with lovely gardens to enjoy in the warmer months. A bar menu is offered and includes anything from baguettes to steaks and lasagne.

When the Coach and Horses is closed, try the **Vineyard Inn** which is about 2 miles north on the old Evesham road. It is popular with ramblers and is open throughout the winter months and here you can indulge in good food throughout the year.
☎ 01386 870217 Website: www.vineyardinn.co.uk

Opening times each day of the week between March and the end of October are from noon to 2.30 pm and from 5 pm until 11 pm. During this summer period, food is available from noon to 2 pm and from 5 pm to 9 pm (no food on Sunday evening).
☎ 01386 870249

1 From the lay-by nearly opposite **Myatt's Field** head down the private road of **Myatt's Field**. At its end turn left and proceed along the waymarked public footpath along the back of houses to reach the B4088. Cross over the road with care and walk along the farm track to the right opposite. This leads over **Harvington Hill** and past some pigsties. Continue along the track (Harvington Lodge will be 150 yards to your right) set to the right of the field hedge for about ½ mile. Shortly after passing under the electricity pylon, bear right towards the waymark which is visible to the right. At the waymarker turn left and stroll along another farm track heading generally north-west. In about 500 yards

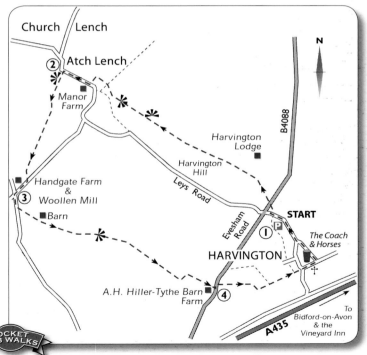

The pigs on Harvington Hill.

bear right away from the farm track on a footpath that leads to a footbridge. Here, the path bends left and then right. Exit the trees and ascend the steepish farm track to the top of the rise. Continue ahead for about 125 yards to a junction of paths and a house. Turn left and stroll along the driveway to the main road in the pretty village of **Atch Lench**. At the main road turn right and stroll through the delightful village, passing by a number of attractive thatched cottages until you reach a right bend in the road.

[2] Turn left and stroll up the hedged footpath to the left of **Corner Cottage**. Go over the stile, pausing to enjoy the view of the **Malvern Hills** to your right. Then proceed along the footpath initially to the right of the field hedge, following the clear waymarker. The footpath will switch to the left-hand side of the hedge and then you go over a footbridge. The footpath continues to the left of the field hedge and you will see **Handgate Farm and Woollen Mill** to the left ahead. Go over the stile to enter the farm garden, bearing left towards a gate set to the right of a large barn; then exit onto the lane. Turn right along the lane until you reach a road.

Harvington Walk 10

Turn left and walk along the grass verge of the road for the next 125 yards. Now cross over the road, pass left through the gap to the right of the farm gate and proceed along the clear farm track. This takes you past a large barn and you continue ahead. After going through another hedge gap, you ascend the next field and proceed beneath the electricity wires. Descend the steep hill and continue along the signed footpath – initially walking to the left of the field hedge and then veering to walk to its right. Soon you are walking on a hedged track, which becomes a grassy track on the left of the hedge, and you will arrive in an orchard area. The path bends left and then right and you walk to the left of the fruit trees. Exit the fruit farm of A.H.Hiller by **Tythe Barn Farm** to arrive on the B4088 road once again.

Turn left and, in 25 yards, cross over the road with great care. Turn right and pass between the buildings opposite into a large apple orchard, walking to the right of the trees for the next 450 yards. **Harvington church** is ahead and you turn right at the fence, then left and then right again. In 60 yards turn left and walk by the side of fenced-off plum trees, descending gently to go over the footbridge and then ascend a fenced footpath towards the village. At the T-junction of footpaths turn right along the hedged footpath that arcs left to arrive on **Stratford Road**. Turn left up the lovely old road where half-timbered and thatched cottages will catch your eye. Bear right towards the church, opposite the **Coach & Horses**. Turn left to return to the start.

Places of interest nearby

Evesham Country Park (4 miles south at the junction of the Evesham bypass and the Stratford road) offers a relaxed shopping experience with its large garden centre and courtyard facilities. After browsing you can explore the 130-acre estate.
☎ *01386 761888*

The Brandy Cask

Pershore is a small market town set amid woodlands and fruit farms near to the river Avon. Reached by a fine 14th-century, six-arch bridge, the town is today best known for its superb Norman abbey. Originally much larger than Worcester Abbey, Pershore Abbey was founded in AD 618 but was largely destroyed at the dissolution – the only part of the original abbey to remain is the choir. Even so the impressive abbey cuts a fine picture with its huge corner turrets and spire pinnacles. In the town, ancient houses and inns line the main streets and the square. This easy stroll starts from Broad Street, then meanders through lovely open countryside and woodland, ascending the edge of the trees to emerge for a fine view of the Malvern Hills.

The abbey is soon reached, followed by a stroll through the picturesque streets to arrive at the Brandy Cask pub. A short walk will take you back to the car park. This is the town where those delicious Pershore plums are grown.

THE PUB

The **Brandy Cask**, on Bridge Street, is a beautiful Georgian building with delightful landscaped gardens stretching down to the river Avon. When built in 1779, it was a liquor vault but today is a very popular pub, with a reputation for good food and a warm welcome. Several real ales are on tap and you will find Dry Blackthorn and Woodpecker ciders. A wide selection of light bites or starters are available, together with a selection of home-made courses providing superb meals. Daily specials are available but booking is required for the popular 3-course Sunday lunch.

Opening times are from 11.30 am to 2.30 pm and 7 pm to 11 pm on weekdays. Saturday it is open from 11.30 am to 3 pm and from 7 pm to 11 pm and on Sundays from noon to 3 pm and from 7 pm to 10.30 pm. Food is available every day between noon and 2 pm and 7 pm to 9 pm.
☎ *01386 552602*

Distance 6 miles.

OS Explorer 190 Malvern Hills. GR 949457.

Starting point Broad Street, Pershore.

Easy walk on good footpaths and farm tracks.

How to get there *Pershore is situated 8½ miles south-east of Worcester. Turn off the A44 on the A4104 into Pershore.*

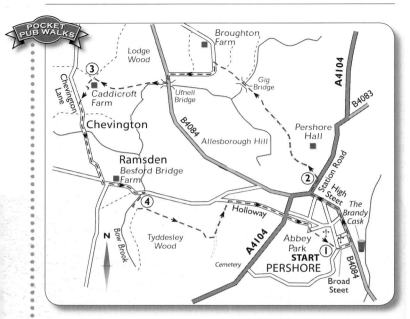

1 Walk to the top of **Broad Street** and then go left along **High Street**, passing the **Pastry Case teashop** on the left. Do spare time to enjoy seeing some of the very fine buildings which include the **Angel Inn** and the **Posting House**, a superb old coaching inn with an elegant façade. The bow windows were once those of the Ship Inn which has been recently converted into three shops. Continue along the pavement of **High Street** until you reach the junction with **Station Road**. Cross over the main road (the B4084) with care and turn right up **Station Road**.

2 After about 200 yards, cross over the road and stroll up **Gig Bridge Lane** opposite. Where the lane arcs right to become **Mount Pleasant**, proceed ahead, ascending a good farm track into open countryside – walk on this fine track for the next ½

mile. As soon as you go over the brow of the hill you will be greeted with a pleasing view towards the **Malvern Hills** and will then descend to reach a footpath that leads over **Gig Bridge**. Ascend right up the next field going over a stile; then stroll along a wide headland, keeping to the left of the field hedges. You will pass by some productive runner bean plantations and then veer right by the hedge through a farm gate onto a lane. Turn left and walk along the lane, passing by **Sharloam Stud** and **Willow Bank Cottage** to arrive at the B4084 road once again. Go left down the pavement of the B4084 for about 100 yards, then cross with care to go over a stile to the right of **Ufnell Bridge**. Descend

Pershore Abbey.

the steps into pastureland and proceed along the clear path to the right of the trees and a small stream. The route continues up the next field, and, after bearing right, go through a hedge gap to walk the right side of the field hedge.

3 Immediately after passing by **Caddicroft Farm**, turn left over a footbridge/stile and take a path to the left of the field hedge. Continue over three further stiles and you will arrive at the drive to the farm that leads to **Chevington Lane**. Turn left and stroll down **Chevington Lane** until you reach a road junction in the hamlet of **Ramsden**, where you turn left and walk along the quiet country road for about 400 yards.

4 Turn right over a stile onto a wide path near to the banks of **Bow Brook**. At the field end, turn left to arrive on the edge of **Tyddesley Wood**, then turn left again and walk up the clear waymarked footpath through the trees. Continue into the open and walk on the well-walked footpath to a track, where you can enjoy a fine panoramic view that embraces the **Malvern Hills**. Turn left and then at **Holloway Road** turn right and descend the residential road to the A4104. Cross over this and stroll down **Newlands** (to the left opposite) to reach the grounds of the superb abbey. Stroll through **Abbey Park** and return to your car.

Places of interest nearby

Pershore Abbey combines outstanding examples of Norman and early English Architecture and is well worth a visit. It is possible to climb the fine tower but you will need to phone in advance.
☎ *01386 561520*

12 Worcestershire Beacon

The Brewers Arms

The Malvern Hills are approximately 8 miles long and rise to 1,394 ft at the Worcestershire Beacon, providing a major landmark for the Midlands. On top of the hills, a medieval 'Shire Ditch' was built between 1287 and 1291 by the red-headed Gilbert de Clare (Earl of Gloucester). It was constructed to divide his hunting forests from those of the Bishop of Hereford. Today 'Shire Ditch' is still clearly visible and the route takes you near part of it before descending into West Malvern. Then

Distance 3¾ miles.

OS Explorer 190 Malvern Hills and Bredon Hill.
GR 763404.

Starting point Pay and display car park (toilets) at the Wyche.

A strenuous walk to the Beacon, then easy stroll along good grass tracks.

How to get there From Malvern take the A449 south towards Ledbury. In about 1 mile bear right up Holy Well Road. Just after passing the Wyche Inn turn right to find the pay and display car park.

you walk on lovely tracks before ascending back to the Wyche car park. The Worcestershire Beacon was an obvious place for a warning beacon and Lord Macaulay, the 19th-century poet, gave the Malverns a central role in this warning chain of fires in his famous poem *The Armada*. In Victorian times there was a camera obscura on the Worcestershire Beacon and until 1989 there was a café at its top. Sadly, the café burnt down; so you may want to take a drink with you if you wish to meander and enjoy the wonderful views.

THE PUB Originally built by Edmund Pitt in the early 1830s, the **Brewers Arms** became a pub in 1872 but suffered a severe fire in 1992. Happily, it has again become the hub of the area and is the local of the celebrated violinist Nigel Kennedy. You are guaranteed good food in this remote but friendly pub and it varies from sandwiches through to steaks, with roasts available on Sundays. Meals can be eaten in the main pub, in a separate restaurant or in the beer gardens in fine weather.

Worcestershire Beacon   Walk 12

Opening times Monday to Saturday are from noon to 3 pm and in the evenings from 6 pm to midnight. On Sunday it is open all day between noon and midnight. Food is served between noon and 3 pm during the week. At weekends food is served between noon and 9 pm (Sunday until 7 pm). If you are an early walker, breakfast is served between 9 am and 11 am.
☎ *01684 568147* **Website** – *www.brewersarmswithaview.co.uk*

1 From the car park, ascend north up the clear tarmac path set to the left of **Shire Ditch**. You can stroll along the ditch but the walking can be uneven and you need to take care not to cause damage, but it does offer a fine view to both the east and west. After a couple of stiff climbs you will arrive at the **Worcestershire Beacon**, which was erected in 1897 to commemorate the 60th year of Queen Victoria's reign and offers a spectacular panorama in all directions. When ready, continue north, descending rather steeply to reach a clear junction of paths with a circular stone waymarker at their centre.

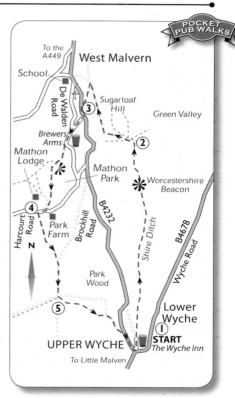

En route through the Malverns Hills.

[2] Follow the **West Malvern** direction (on top of the stone) and walk on the good track towards the village. There are fine views over West Malvern as you descend the easy track. All too soon you will be approaching buildings and, at the junction, turn left, passing a cottage and then houses until you reach the B4232 in the village.

[3] Cross over the road with care and continue down **Park Road** opposite. In about 200 yards you will see **De Walden Road** coming in from your right and soon ahead you will see the driveway to **Mathon Lodge**. Here bear left and then turn left after the white cottage to ascend a slope up to the **Brewers Arms**. Retrace your steps to **Blackheath Way** and then bear left

down the tarmac track into the Mathon estate. Soon you will go over a stile to walk down a beautiful tree-lined driveway with views of the **Malvern Hills** up to your left. A final stile takes you down to **Harcourt Road** where you turn right to reach the road corner.

4 Turn left and cross over the quiet road to walk down a clear driveway that leads to several houses. Proceed over a couple of stiles and continue southwards, walking on a clear grass track set to the right of the field hedge. Go over a couple of stiles, the second of which takes you left onto a lane called **Brockhill Road**. You will pass an old lime kiln and then will reach a junction of paths and tracks near a cottage.

5 Turn left, following the footpath signs that take you to the right of the cottage, and ascend towards trees. Another stile leads onto a hedged footpath that skirts to the left of another house. This is lovely walking on a clear footpath that soon opens out and you will reach a junction of paths. Continue ahead, bearing right up an earth lane past houses. At its top you will arrive at the B4232 road once again. Here, turn right and stroll along the pavement for about 100 yards, then turn left and ascend some steps, following the footpath back to your car.

Places of interest nearby

Barnard's Green House (1 mile east) is a Grade II listed house, dating from 1635. It is surrounded by a wonderful garden that it is possible to explore, containing some fine mature gardens and a superb vegetable garden.
☎ *01684 574446*

Malvern Splash Leisure Complex (also 1 mile east) includes a beach area, flume and a wave machine, as well as sauna and sunbed facilities.
☎ *01684 893423*

13 British Camp

The Malvern Hills Hotel

he Malvern Hills were formed more than 600 million years ago during volcanic activity caused by heating and changes below the earth's surface. The medieval 'Shire Ditch' on top of the hills was built by the Earl of Gloucester in such a way as to allow the Bishop of Hereford's deer to get over onto the Earl's land but unable to return to the Bishop's forests. Today Shire Ditch is still clearly visible and runs virtually the whole length of the Malverns. This route takes you near part of this historic ditch and along part of the Worcestershire Way path. The Herefordshire Beacon (338m) was pronounced by the celebrated 17th-century diarist, John Evelyn, to be 'one of the goodliest vistas in England'.

Distance 4¾ miles.

OS Explorer 190 Malvern Hills and Bredon Hill. GR 763404

Starting Point Pay and display car park (toilets) at British Camp.

A fairly easy walk with a more strenuous stretch around Herefordshire Beacon

How to get there *From Malvern, take the A449 road towards Ledbury. At the peak of the Malvern Hills, park in the large car park at British Camp.*

THE PUB

There has been an inn on the site of the **Malvern Hills Hotel** for more than half a millennium. A wide selection of home-cooked food is always available, as is a great range of real ales. The lovely food varies from bar snacks and sandwiches through to full à la carte meals. Look out for the daily specials on the blackboard.

Opening times are from 11 am to 11 pm Monday to Saturday. On Sunday the hotel is open from noon to 10.30 pm. Food is available from noon to 2.15 pm Monday to Friday and from noon to 2.30 pm on Saturday and Sunday.
☎ *01684 540690*

1 From the car park at **British Camp**, cross the A449 road with care. The toilets are on the left as you walk past the **Malvern Hills Hotel**. Just past the hotel, bear right off the B4232 onto a clear stone path. The path leads through **Wynds Point car park** and ascends to **Shire Ditch**, where you bear left to take the footpath to the left of the ridge. There are fine views to the west

as the path arcs to the left. Take the first left fork and descend gently to cross over the B4232 road. Now take the lane opposite, passing by **The Kettle Sings** – a pleasant place to have a cup of tea and enjoy the view. Continue along the quiet lane for about 325 yards to reach a bend in the lane.

2 Turn left over a stile to descend through trees on a footpath that arcs left for some 440 yards to reach a path junction. Here there is a pleasing view of the valley below. Turn right for about 65 yards; then bear left over a stile, descending two fields and walking by the right field hedge to go over a further stile. At the bottom of the second field, turn left onto the **Worcestershire Way**. Proceed ahead, passing through a gateway and at the end of the next field bear left, ascending over a stile before continuing to the right of the hedge. The footpath soon veers right and ascends (the Kettle Sings café can be seen up to the left) to a stile into trees. Turn right and descend to a stile into open pastureland, where once again there are views of the **Malvern Hills** to the left and **Herefordshire Beacon** ahead. The **Worcestershire Way** arcs to the side of a coppice that you enter at the second stile. After descending

The Malvern Hills near Herefordshire Beacon.

through the coppice you exit via a stile near an attractive cottage called **Spindrift** – those views are back yet again. Bear left along the cottage drive until you arrive at the road in **Evendine**.

3 Head right along the road for about 120 yards, then cross over and bear left along the waymarked path opposite. The footpath crosses a cultivated field to go over a stile and path and continues south over several farm fields. Go over the stile by a permissive path waymarker and turn right, walking on the other side of the hedge to a field corner stile. Ignore the finger post directing left up to **British Camp** and continue ahead to a further stile into **Hatfield Coppice**. Ascend the track through the pleasant coppice, passing through a gate to reach the busy A449 road.

Turn left along the side of the road for about 25 yards; then cross over with care and take the **Worcestershire Way** opposite. You pass **Hill Farm**, walking to the right of **Herefordshire Beacon**. About 275 yards beyond the small farm you will reach a gate.

4 Just before this gate, leave the **Worcestershire Way** by going left and begin a zigzag ascent of **Herefordshire Beacon** for another memorable panoramic view.

The Herefordshire Beacon (338 m/1,111 ft) contains one of the country's finest Iron Age contour forts. The site is believed to have been a fortified hill-town of some 2,000 people living in timber and mud huts in the third century BC, when the natural slopes of the hill were used to advantage in the construction of the defensive ramparts. Initially the view embraces Camp Reservoir and later the main range of the Malverns, including Worcestershire Beacon.

After going over the top of the beacon you will descend north-east on a clear path (in part with concrete steps to protect the hillside) back to the car park at **British Camp**.

Places of interest nearby

Little Malvern Court (½ mile east) is a 15th-century building that was once part of the Little Malvern Priory church. It is an interesting building with ten acres of beautiful gardens to explore.
☎ *01684 892988*

Ledbury (5 miles south-west) is a pretty market town. The poet, John Masefield, who described it as 'pleasant to the sight, fair and half-timbered houses black and white', was born in the town.

14 **Broadway Tower**

The Horse and Hound

Often referred to as the 'jewel of the Cotswolds' and the 'show village of England', Broadway has a long open street, lined with graceful 16th- and 17th-century houses built in wonderful honey-coloured Cotswold stone. There are thatched roofs, steep gables thrusting out above the roof-line of dormer windowed cottages, and there is a fine village green. The 16th-century Lygon Arms Hotel, prominently positioned in the High Street, boasts Charles I and Oliver Cromwell among its past guests. As you ascend the High Street from the green there is a dead-end road containing more beautiful Cotswold stone houses before you reach the famous Fish Hill, where many a lorry has been stuck in inclement weather. Standing imperiously over the village in a 30-acre country park is the 65 ft Broadway Tower, offering spectacular views over twelve counties. This walk takes you up part of the

Cotswold Way to visit the tower. The route then heads back through the country park into beautiful countryside where, in spring, there are bluebells and wild flowers to admire.

THE PUB The **Horse and Hound** 'picturesque from the outside, wonderfully alive on the inside' is a historic Cotswold stone inn where you can enjoy the best that England's largest Area of Outstanding Natural Beauty has to offer. You will receive a warm welcome and apart from facilities for passing walkers the inn offers five rooms for hire. Who can resist the mushroom stroganoff or perhaps an item from the specials board.

Opening times are 11 am to 11 pm Monday to Saturday and from noon to 10.30 pm on Sunday. Food is available between noon and 3 pm and 6 pm to 9 pm Monday to Saturday, and from noon to 3.30 pm on Sunday.
☎ *01386 852287 www.thehorseandhound.co.uk*

[1] From the car park walk past the back of the toilet block and proceed along the public footpath that will lead you into the

Distance 4 miles.

OS Outdoor Leisure 45 The Cotswolds. GR 096379.

Starting point The pay and display car park in Leamington Road, Broadway.

A hill ascent, then easy walking on good paths.

How to get there From the A44, enter Broadway on Leamington Road. You will find the pay and display car park on your left just before reaching the High Street.

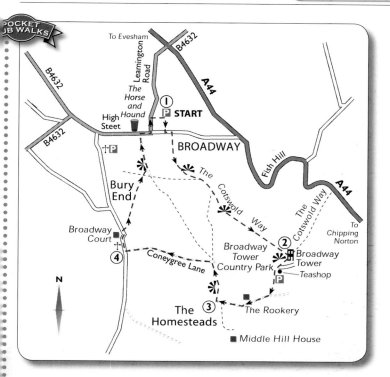

High Street in **Broadway**. Cross the main road and turn left, then right, where you will see the **Cotswold Way** sign. Enter the narrow lane that leads to open land below **Broadway Hill**. After going over stiles you will pass through a small yard into pastureland and into beautiful open Cotswold countryside. Follow the **Cotswold Way**, going generally south-east as you cross a stream to reach a hurdle and stile. Now you will begin the ascent of **Broadway Hill**, but do pause at the viewing seat to enjoy the fine retrospective view of Broadway, Burhill and the Vale of Evesham towards Bredon Hill. Continue the ascent, going over several stiles as you walk to the right of a Cotswold stone wall and soon **Broadway Tower** will come into view on the skyline ahead. You will arrive by a high wire fence near the tower.

2 Leave the **Cotswold Way** by turning right into **Broadway Country Park** via a tall kissing gate and visit the magnificent tower – the wonderful view from here embraces the Vale of Evesham, Broadway, Bredon Hill and the Malverns, extending to the Shropshire Hills and the Black Mountains. Continue past the tower and exit the park by another tall kissing gate. Now go right along the park drive, passing the café in the country park

Broadway Tower.

complex and go through a small hand gate into pastureland. Bear left to reach a stile onto a farm lane. Turn right and descend the lane, passing the entrance drive to **The Rookery** and continue ahead along a track that will take you into the trees.

At the track junction, turn right and walk generally northwards. Bear left by an attractive cottage and walk on the lovely footpath towards trees. Turn right and then left to descend **Coneygree Lane**. If you walk along the footpath in the trees to the right of the main track in spring, you can tiptoe through a carpet of wonderful bluebells.

At the bottom of the lane you will see the church across the road opposite. Turn right along quiet **Snowshill Road**, passing the church and the superb Cotswold stone building of **Broadway Court**. In a further 150 yards look out for a waymarker in the field corner to your right and go over this. Walk up the good footpath across lovely pastureland, following the direction of the waymarkers over several fields. Soon you will arrive in **Broadway** to emerge in the **High Street**, opposite the **Horse and Hound** pub. Take in the atmosphere of one of the most photographed streets in the U.K. and when you are ready stroll up **High Street** and turn left into **Leamington Road** to return to the car park.

Places of interest nearby

Snowshill Manor (National Trust) is 2½ miles south-west of Broadway and the home of thousands of fascinating treasures collected by architect and craftsman Charles Paget Wade. There are terraces, byres and ponds to explore in the lovely gardens.
☎ 01386 852410

The Star Inn

Ashton under Hill is such an appropriate name for this most attractive village set beneath the beautiful Bredon Hill. The village is in a conservation area and there are many early black and white thatched cottages to admire. The main road through Ashton displays a wonderful mixture of seventeen listed buildings, including a Georgian house. The sub-post office is in a 400-year-old thatched cottage. This exhilarating circuit offers the opportunity to climb one of the most beautiful hills on the edge of the Cotswolds and to visit some of the delightful villages that surround it. Seek a day of good weather to appreciate a super view of the vale of Evesham and the Cotswolds and to enjoy refreshment at the Star Inn on your return. Bredon Hill is a walkers' paradise and you may well be tempted to come back and walk to the very top.

THE
PUB

The 500-year-old **Star Inn** was originally three cottages. Every day there are two or three guest ales to taste and Strongbow cider is on tap. A good mix of home-cooked food is always available from the blackboard – the steak and ale pie is a particular favourite. It is important to book for Sunday lunch. Walkers who are customers may leave their cars in the pub car park whilst they walk.

Opening times are noon to 2 pm (to 3 pm on Saturday and until 4 pm on Sunday) and 7 pm to 11 pm, (closed Monday lunchtime and also all day Tuesday and Wednesday during the winter months).
☎ *01386 881325*

From the **Star Inn**, walk up through the pretty village for nearly ½ mile, passing attractive half-timbered cottages (some thatched) – note the white thatched Old Post House on the right. Towards the top of the village, turn left up **Cotton's Lane**. After passing a number of country cottages you will be ascending a driveway

Distance 4¼ miles.

Starting point Ashton under Hill, near the Star Inn.

OS Explorer 190 The Malverns. GR 997377.

Easy walking, with one hill ascent.

How to get there *Ashton under Hill is 25 miles south-east of Worcester. From Junction 9 of the M5 take the A46 towards Evesham. From the roundabout on the A46, head towards Evesham for about 6 miles, then turn left into Station Road. In about ½ mile turn right to Ashton under Hill.*

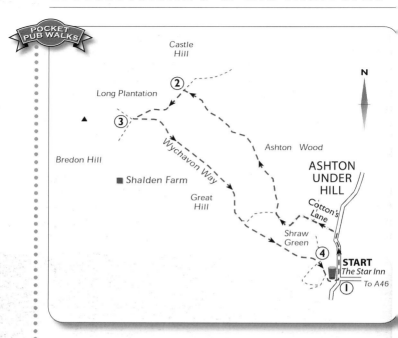

towards **Shaw Green** and will be able to enjoy a nice view over **Ashton under Hill** to your left. The drive bends left and then right, then passes between farm buildings where you will reach a farm gate and a cattle grid. Proceed through the gate and ascend the hedged track, passing through a second gate before veering right into delightful open countryside. Aim for the gate in the top left corner of the next field; then continue ahead on the other side of the hedge, going through a gate so as to walk to the left of **Ashton Wood** – do this for its whole length, progressing through two further gates. Continue by the hedge, maintaining your north-easterly direction through two gates, and then go to the right of the hedge to reach a final gate in the middle of the fence ahead. There are fine views to the right. Proceed ahead over the crest of the hill and go over the stile in the far fence.

Turn left and ascend the **Wychavon Way** route to a gate at the bottom end of **Long Plantation**. Ascend the bridlepath track through the plantation to a gate at its very top and open countryside at 917 ft (280m) – to the right is the peak of **Bredon Hill** at 926 ft (283m). The magnificent views from Bredon take in a large slice of the Midlands and, in clear conditions, the Welsh mountains can be seen. The summit is a magnificent viewing point and it is not surprising that it was used as a fort in prehistoric times.

Turn left following the **Wychavon Way** along a clear path between the plantation and a wire fence. Walk on this path for about ¾ mile, passing through a gate by the end of the plantation. Continue to the right of the stone wall, bearing right to a bridleway signpost and go through a gate, then descend

Alabaster effigies in St Mary's church.

between the hill banks to a waymarker, bearing slightly right to reach a metal gate – the views remain superb all the way down the hill. Descend the next field, going over a stile and maintaining your direction over a further stile. Proceed across the middle of the next field, passing two solitary trees to a post and then a track.

4 Continue to follow the waymarkers and descend steeply, aiming towards **St Barbara's parish church** in **Ashton under Hill**. Cross a track before going over two stiles to reach a kissing gate in the bottom corner of the field. Enter the churchyard, exiting via the fine church lychgate. Turn left to find your car – the **Star Inn** will be on the left.

Places of interest nearby

Elmley Castle, to the north-west of Ashton, is a most beautiful and peaceful village. Visit the church of St Mary the Virgin because the transept contains remarkable monuments, all wonderfully preserved in alabaster. There is a large tomb chest with effigies of Sir William Savage, Sir Giles (his son) and Lady Catherine Savage (his wife). Lady Catherine, who is buried at Malvern Priory church, carries an infant daughter born after the death of her father. At her feet is the head of a unicorn, at the men's feet lions. Four sons kneel on an 'extension' to the tomb, at their parents' feet – truly amazing.